Owls

Written by Adrienne Mason

Illustrated by Nancy Gray Ogle

KIDS CAN PRESS

WILDLIFE SERIES

Kids Can Press

For Bob — AM
For my daughter, Lindsay — NGO

I would like to thank the following bird experts for their manuscript review and consultation:
Barry Booth, Corvus Environmental Consulting; Dick Cannings, Consulting Biologist for Bird Studies
Canada; and David Fraser, Endangered Species Specialist for the British Columbia government.
As always, it was a pleasure to work with the wonderful team from Kids Can Press.
Special thanks to Nancy Gray Ogle for bringing my words to life.

Kids Can Press acknowledges the financial support of
the Government of Ontario, through the Ontario Media
Development Corporation's Ontario Book Initiative; the
Ontario Arts Council; the Canada Council for the Arts;
and the Government of Canada, through the BPIDP, for
our publishing activity.

Published in Canada by
Kids Can Press Ltd.
29 Birch Avenue
Toronto, ON M4V 1E2

Published in the U.S. by
Kids Can Press Ltd.
2250 Military Road
Tonawanda, NY 14150

www.kidscanpress.com

Edited by Stacey Roderick
Designed by Marie Bartholomew
Printed and bound in China

The hardcover edition of this book is smyth sewn
casebound.
The paperback edition of this book is limp sewn with a
drawn-on cover.

CM 04 0 9 8 7 6 5 4 3 2 1
CM PA 04 0 9 8 7

**National Library of Canada Cataloguing in
Publication Data**

Mason, Adrienne
   Owls / written by Adrienne Mason ; illustrated by
Nancy Gray Ogle.

(Kids Can Press wildlife series)
Includes index.

ISBN 978-1-55337-623-1 (bound)
ISBN 978-1-55337-624-8 (pbk.)

1. Owls — Juvenile literature. I. Ogle, Nancy Gray
II. Title. III. Series.

QL696.S8M34 2004   j598.9'7   C2003-906975-3

Kids Can Press is a *corus* ™ Entertainment company

Contents

Owls

Owls are birds with large eyes, big round heads and fluffy feathers. They glide silently through the sky with their long, wide wings.

Owls are birds of prey — birds that hunt other animals for food. Birds of prey have hooked beaks and sharp claws to help them catch their food. Most owls rest during the day and hunt at night because they eat animals that are active at night.

The largest owl is the great gray owl.
It is almost as tall as a kitchen counter.

The smallest owl, the elf owl, would fit in the palm of your hand.

OWL FACT

Owls have eyes that face forward, just like your eyes do. The eyes of most other birds are on the sides of their head.

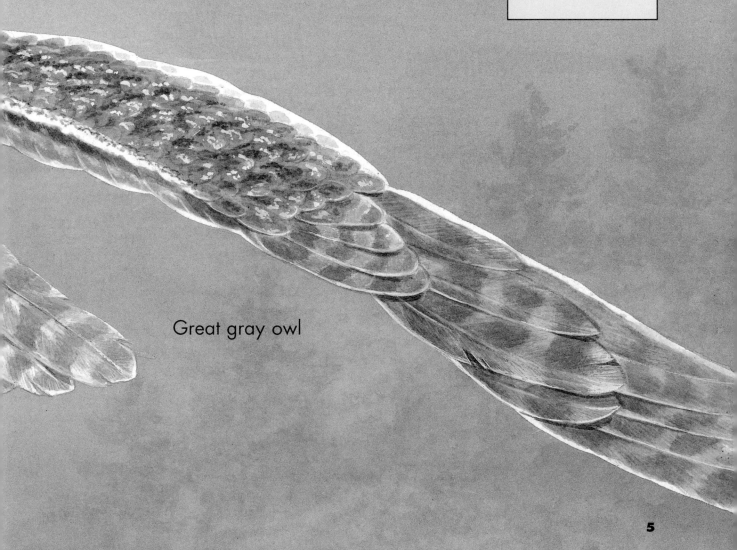

Great gray owl

Kinds of owls

There are about 180 species of owls around the world. They belong to one of two groups: barn owls or typical owls.

Barn owl

Barns owls have heart-shaped faces, long legs and light-colored feathers. There is only one species of barn owl in North America.

Great horned owl

Most typical owls have a mix of brown, gray, black and reddish feathers. This makes them look streaked. Typical owls have flat, wide faces. Some have tufts of feathers on their head that look like ears or horns. There are 18 types of typical owls in North America.

Where owls live

Owls live in forests, on prairies, in deserts and marshes and even in cities. They stay where there is plenty of food and where there are places to rest and hide. Owls usually live alone or with one other owl, but some species live in larger groups.

Many owls live in the same place all year. Some owls, such as the short-eared owl, move from one place to another as the seasons change to find food. This is called migrating.

Some owls, such as the burrowing owl, live near fields.

The long-eared owl and many other owls live in forests. Their streaked feathers help them hide in the trees.

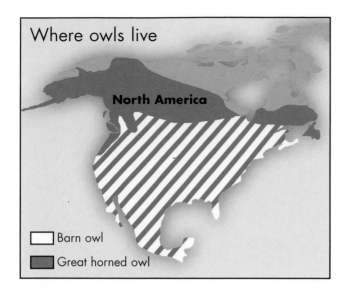

Where owls live

North America

☐ Barn owl
▨ Great horned owl

OWL FACT

A group of owls is called a parliament.

Barn owls can live in barns or other buildings, but they also live in caves or holes in trees.

Tiny elf owls live in the desert. They sometimes find shelter inside cactus plants.

Owl food

Owls wait quietly without moving until they see or hear their prey. Then they swoop down and grab the animal with their needle-sharp talons, or claws.

What an owl eats depends on the owl's size. Large owls eat mice and other rodents, birds and even rabbits. Smaller owls also eat rodents and small birds, as well as insects such as grasshoppers, moths and beetles.

Owls swallow small prey whole. If the prey is large, owls kill it with a bite to the neck. Then they tear the animal apart and eat the pieces.

Snowy owl

In one year a barn owl can catch 2000 rats and mice.

Owls can't digest all of the parts of their prey. About eight hours after eating they will cough up a dry pellet. Inside the pellet are the fur, teeth and bones of their last meal.

11

Owl bodies

An owl's body is made for silent flying and hunting. This eastern screech owl is one type of typical owl.

Eyes

Large eyes help owls find food, even in the dark. Special clear eyelids clean and protect their eyes.

Beak

A short, hooked beak is used to grip and kill prey.

Ear tufts

Ear tufts are bunches of feathers that are raised or lowered to show fear, anger or excitement. They do not help owls hear.

Ears

Small ear slits help owls locate their prey, even when they can't see it.

Neck

Extra neck bones allow owls to twist their heads so far around that they can look over their backs.

Feathers

Fluffy feathers next to their skin keep owls warm. Large, strong outer wing feathers are for flying.

Wings

Long, wide wings help owls glide as they hunt.

Bones

Owls' bones are hollow. This makes their skeletons light for easier flying.

Feet

Strong toes with sharp talons are used to catch and hold prey. The outer toe can swivel around from front to back. This helps the owl keep a strong grip on squirming prey.

How owls use sight and sound

Owls have keen sight and hearing to help them hunt, even when it is dark.

Owls have huge eyes that let in lots of light to help them see at night. Owls cannot move their eyes from side to side. Owls bob their heads up and down and from side to side to see better. Their flexible necks also help owls see behind themselves.

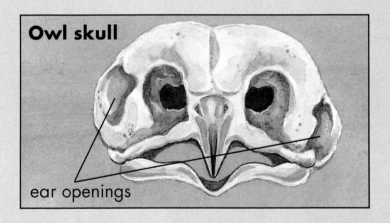

Owl skull

ear openings

Owls can hear so well that they can even hear prey that is under leaves or snow. Some owls have one ear that is higher, larger and points in a different direction from the other, so they hear a sound in each ear at a slightly different time. This helps owls locate exactly where sounds are coming from.

OWL FACT

A great gray owl can hear a mouse under the snow from 30 m (100 ft.) away.

Northern saw-whet owl

How owls fly

Owls are strong fliers and can travel long distances, but most owl flights are short. Owls tend to stay in one territory, or area, so they do not need to fly too far.

Owls fly quietly to swoop silently down on their prey. Silent flying also allows owls to hear their prey while they are moving toward it. Owls will glide just above the ground as they look and listen for food.

Once a year, owls slowly lose and re-grow their feathers. This is called molting. Molting replaces damaged feathers.

Boreal owl

It takes about three months for an owl to molt.

The edges of an owl's wing feathers look like a comb. The spaces help muffle, or quiet, the sound of air moving over an owl's wing.

Owl nests

Owls do not build nests. Instead, they lay their eggs in a hole in a tree, on a cliff or just on the ground. Some owls use the old nests of crows or other large birds. Barn owls nest in barns or other buildings. One species of owl, the burrowing owl, lays its eggs in holes in the ground made by tortoises or prairie dogs.

Owls nest where there is lots of food nearby. Once a pair of owls has chosen their nesting site, they let other owls know. They claim their territory by hooting, screeching or whistling. Sometimes owls will attack intruders that come into their territory.

OWL FACT

Some owls will lay more than ten eggs in a nest.

Snowy owl

Baby owls

Most mother owls lay three or four round white eggs in the spring. The mother owl sits on the eggs to keep them warm. The father protects the nest and brings food to the female. The eggs take about 30 days to hatch.

The mother owl lays one egg at a time, waiting a day or so in between so the eggs do not hatch all at once. When a baby owl is ready to hatch, it uses a tiny egg tooth on its beak to chip open the eggshell.

Baby owls are called owlets. Owlets are born with their eyes closed. They are weak and helpless.

The first baby to hatch will usually grow more quickly than its brothers and sisters. It will get the most food and attention from its parents. The last baby to hatch often starves because it does not get as much food.

Barn owl and owlets

OWL FACT

In years when there is a lot of food in an owl's territory, more owlets survive.

How owls grow and learn

At first, owlets stay with their mother in the nest while their father brings them food. The parents tear the food into small pieces for the owlets. The owlets grow quickly, and soon the mother also needs to leave the nest to help catch food for them.

Owlets first grow fluffy feathers, called down, which keep them warm. When the owlets are about three weeks old, longer feathers begin to grow. As they get older and larger, the owlets will hop away from the nest to stretch and flap their wings.

Parents teach the owlets to fly by tempting them out of the nest with food. When they are about a month old, the owlets begin to practice flying and hunting, but they still need their parents' help to find enough food.

In late summer or fall, the owlets leave their parents to find their own territories.

Great horned owlets

OWL FACT

When owls are as young as one year old, they will use hoots, whistles and other calls to attract a mate.

How owls protect themselves

Adult owls have few predators. But they must defend their owlets and feeding territories from other owls and birds of prey.

Owls use hoots, whistles and screams to warn unwanted visitors away from their territories. They will also attack with their sharp talons.

Owlets and adult owls make themselves look larger if an enemy comes too close. They open their wings, puff up their feathers, snap their beaks and hiss.

The color and shape of owls make them difficult to see. During the day, an owl keeps its feathers close to its body so that it is hidden in the forest. At night, the owl relaxes and puffs out its feathers.

Short-eared owl

Pygmy owls have two dark patches, or false eyes, on the back of their head. False eyes make these tiny owls seem larger and scare enemies away.

Owls and people

Many owls live near people, but sometimes the actions of humans hurt owls. In the past, people often shot owls because they thought owls were pests. Chemicals used on fields also poisoned mice and other owl food. The poisoned food harmed the owls and their young. It made the owls' eggs soft so the shells cracked before it was time for the owlets to hatch. The poisons could also kill the adult owls.

Today, the main threat to owls is the loss of their habitat, the places where owls live. Forests are cut down and cities are built over meadows and marshes. It is hard for owls to survive without enough space to find food and to nest.

Owls help people by controlling the numbers of mice, rats and insects. Many people know this and are trying to help owls by putting up special boxes where owls can hide and nest. Other people are working to protect owl habitat.

Burrowing owls and spotted owls are endangered species. They are endangered because they are losing their habitat.

Barred owl

Owls of the world

Owls live on every continent in the world except Antarctica.
Here are just a few types of owls.

Pearl-spotted owl

White-faced
scops owl

Collared scops owl

Fish owl

Australian
masked owl

Barking owl

Europe

Eagle owl

Barn owl

North America

Northern pygmy owl

Northern hawk owl

Boreal owl

South America

Black-capped screech owl

Spectacled owl

Owl signs

Since owls are often out at night, it can be difficult to see them. It is usually easier to hear their hoots, screeches or whistles. The trick to finding owls is to know where they live.

People look for owls where there are a lot of mice and other types of owl food. Owls can also be found by looking for piles of their pellets. Pellets are dropped below an owl's nest or perch.

Some people can imitate the call of an owl. Or they might use a tape recorder to play an owl's call. If an owl is nearby, it might call back. The owl thinks that there is another owl in its territory.

Words to know

bird of prey: a bird with a hooked beak and talons that hunts other animals for its food

egg tooth: a sharp piece on an owlet's beak used for pecking out of its shell

endangered species: a species that has so few animals left that the species may not survive

habitat: the place where an animal lives

migrate: to travel from one place to another

molting: to lose old feathers that are replaced by new ones

owlet: a baby owl

pellet: a dry packet of fur and bones that is coughed up by an owl after it has eaten

prey: an animal that is hunted for food

rodent: an animal whose front teeth never stop growing, such as a beaver, squirrel, rat and mouse

talon: the claw of an owl or other bird of prey

territory: the area where an animal lives that the animal defends from intruders

Index